Lerner Wildlife Library

Animals of the TEMPERATE FORESTS

written by Sylvia A. Johnson

illustrated by Alcuin C. Dornisch

Lerner Publications Company
Minneapolis, Minnesota

LIBRARY OF CONGRESS CATALOGING IN PUBLICATION DATA

Johnson, Sylvia A.
   Animals of the temperate forests.

   (Lerner Wildlife Library)
   SUMMARY: Explores the physical characteristics and habits of ten animals living in the temperate forest—the raccoon, otter, beaver, moose, porcupine, flying squirrel, red fox, koala, European brown bear, and white-tailed deer.

   1. Forest fauna—Juvenile literature. 2. Mammals—Juvenile literature. [1. Forest animals. 2. Animals] I. Dornisch, Alcuin C. II. Title.

QL112.J57 1976   599'.09'0912   75-27757
ISBN 0-8225-1276-9

Published simultaneously in Canada by
J. M. Dent & Sons (Canada) Ltd., Don Mills, Ontario

Manufactured in the United States of America

International Standard Book Number: 0-8225-1276-9
Library of Congress Catalog Card Number: 75-27757

Contents

Animals of the TEMPERATE FORESTS

Hard-working beavers and playful otters; slow-moving porcupines and bounding deer; moose with branching antlers and foxes with bushy tails: these are some of the fascinating creatures that make their homes in the world's temperate forests. The animals of the temperate forest live among the trees and plants of woodlands areas in the temperate regions of North America, Europe, Asia, and Australia. These woodlands vary according to the climate and the soil found in the different areas. North America, for example, has several different kinds of temperate forests, some made up only of *deciduous* trees (those whose leaves fall in winter), others only of evergreens, and still others of both kinds of trees. Despite such differences, however, most temperate forests have many things in common.

The unique nature of the temperate forest is closely related to the pattern of seasonal change that exists in the temperate regions of the world. In the great forests of the tropical regions, it is always summer, but in the temperate forests, seasons come and go in a yearly cycle of change and growth. The stages of this cycle can be seen most clearly in the trees and plants of the deciduous forest. When the spring sun penetrates the forest, the bare branches of the deciduous trees produce fresh green leaves, and colorful flowering plants burst into bloom on the forest floor. During the long, warm days of summer, the green leaves form a thick canopy overhead, and the plants on the ground live in their shade. In autumn, the leaves of the deciduous trees change color and fall, and the forest is once again open to the sky. Winter brings snow and silence to the forest world, and the promise of a return to active life in the spring.

The seasonal changes in the trees and plants of the temperate forest may seem simple and inevitable to most human observers, but scientists know that such changes are brought about in very complicated ways. They seem to be set in motion by the internal "biological clocks" that regulate the activities of all living things, plants and animals. These "clocks" are, in turn, affected by changes in the environment—by the yearly increases and decreases in the hours of daylight, by rising and falling temperatures, by changes in amounts of moisture. In spring, the hours of daylight become gradually longer, and trees respond to this change by producing buds and leaves. In the same way, the shorter days of autumn set off the complex internal mechanism that causes tree leaves to fall.

The same kinds of environmental changes affect the animals of the forest. As the hours of daylight increase in spring, migrating birds return to their forest homes and prepare for the season of mating and nesting. Hibernating animals, their winter sleep having run its course, emerge from their hiding places and begin to search for food. When autumn brings shorter days, these same animals begin to prepare for hibernation by consuming large quantities of food to build up a nourishing layer of fat on their bodies. Animals that do not hibernate respond to the season's message by storing food for winter use or by growing heavy coats of hair and fur.

Whatever the season, the animals of the temperate forest live in close relationship with their environment, responding to its continuing changes and sharing in its varied resources. Because the members of this natural community must share not only resources but also living space, each animal has its own special place in the structure of forest life. The framework of this structure is made up of layers of vegetation, and it is within these layers that the various animals of the forest make their homes. The topmost layer of a mature temperate forest is the *canopy*, which consists of the tops of the forest's tallest trees. Exposed to intense sunlight, the green leaves of the canopy grow thick and lush; many leaf-eating insects and insect-eating birds make their homes here. Squirrels, too, are at home in the canopy, as well as in the next layer of the forest, the *understory*. Smaller trees make up this level of vegetation—either young trees of the same species as the full-grown canopy trees or different species that do not reach such heights.

*Temperate Forests
of the World*

Below the understory is the *shrub* layer of forest growth, consisting of woody plants such as rhododendron and viburnum. Many small animals—chipmunks, mice, certain kinds of birds—find shelter and food among the branches of the forest shrubs. Many other small creatures, as well as larger animals such as foxes and deer, can be found in the lowest level of forest vegetation, the *herb* layer. Grasses, wild flowers, ferns, and mosses are all considered herbs in scientific terms, and the layer of life that they create is one of the most active in the temperate forest. Beneath the herb layer is the *forest floor*, which is littered with dead leaves in autumn and busy with the activities of microscopic organisms all year round.

Each layer of the temperate forest, from the sunlit canopy to the shadowy forest floor, provides a home for a great variety of animals. In the following pages, you will have an opportunity to meet a few of these fascinating forest creatures.

Raccoon

The raccoon (*Procyon lotor*) is one of the most familiar wild animals of North America. This mischievious and intelligent relative of the panda lives in every state in the United States except Alaska and Hawaii. Although raccoons are most at home in the woodlands and fields, they have proved themselves able to adapt to changing environmental conditions with great ease. Naturalists report that there are raccoons living and thriving today in the urban setting of New York City. In their more normal surroundings, raccoons usually make their homes in hollow trees or in rock-sheltered dens. The animals sleep throughout the day, either rolled up in little balls or flat on their backs, with their front feet covering their eyes. At night the raccoon scrambles out of its den and goes in search of food to satisfy its enormous appetite. A raccoon's diet is both animal and vegetable— fresh-water creatures such as crayfish, frogs, and clams, fruits and berries of all kinds, nuts and grains. Whenever there is water available, raccoons usually wash their food several times before eating it—even food that they have just taken out of the water. No one knows the explanation for this mysterious behavior.

European Brown Bear

European brown bears once lived in forests all over Europe, but today there are not many of these huge animals left. Their numbers have decreased as vast stretches of European woodland have been cleared away to make room for human progress. Now the European brown bear can be found only in a few forested mountain areas in central Europe, in the Pyrenees Mountains between Spain and France, and in the cold northern territory of Lapland. In these areas, the European brown bear lives the same life that its ancestors lived when they roamed the great forests of an earlier period. A solitary creature, like all bears, the European brown bear spends most of the spring, summer, and fall searching for food. Its diet is extremely varied, consisting of such things as fruits, nuts, roots, grasses, insects, fish, amphibians, and small mammals. As winter approaches, the European brown bear eats as much as it can in preparation for the period of winter sleep that is to come. Like most other bears except the polar bear, the European brown bear spends the winter months dozing in a shallow cave or a hollow log. The animal does not actually hibernate but instead enters a state of sleep during which its body temperature, breathing rate, and heartbeat fall only a little below normal. It is during this period of inactivity that the female European brown bear has her cubs—usually twins. The young bears are born blind and hairless; they are tiny creatures, often weighing less than a pound at birth. Nourished by their mother's milk, the cubs grow rapidly during the two months that they spend in the den. By the time spring arrives, they are ready to leave their birthplace and to begin their education in the ways of wilderness life.

Porcupine

Many animals of the woodlands have ways of protecting themselves against their enemies, but none is quite so well equipped for self-defense as the porcupine (genus *Erethizon*). This slow-moving rodent is covered by a blanket of sharp, hollow quills that spell trouble for almost any animal foolish enough to attack. A porcupine cannot throw its quills, as some people believe, but it can raise and lower them. When an enemy approaches, the porcupine raises its quills, lowers its body to the ground, and puts its face between its front legs. It does this to protect its tender face and belly, which are not covered by quills. If an attacker persists in annoying the porcupine, the animal thrashes out with its tail, planting hundreds of sharp quills in the enemy. The quills have barbs on the ends and, once implanted, are almost impossible to pull out. Instead, they work themselves inward, causing the victim severe pain. Death may even result if the quills produce infection or if they eventually pierce a vital organ. Despite this danger, there are some animals that are not put off by the porcupine's bristly defense system. Wolves, mountain lions, and bears can survive a quill attack. Even more important, these hunters know how to find a porcupine's unprotected spot by flipping the animal over and exposing its quill-less underside. Left alone, the porcupine itself will never attack another animal. Its diet is strictly vegetarian— flowers and leaves during the spring and summer, tree bark during the fall and winter. After the first snow has fallen, a porcupine will often climb up into a birch or pine tree and spend most of the winter there, gnawing away at the tree's tender inner bark.

Flying Squirrel

Despite its name, the flying squirrel (*Glaucomys volans*) does not actually fly. Instead, this member of the squirrel family glides from tree to tree by spreading the fur-covered folds of skin that grow along its sides. Before launching itself from a tree branch, a flying squirrel tilts its head from side to side, apparently measuring by sight the angle and distance of its glide. After this preparation, the little mammal leaps into the air with its legs spread out at right angles to its body. The path of its glide is downward at first, then level, and finally upward, as the squirrel comes in for a landing. It lands on target with its face turned toward the sky and its legs spread. A flying squirrel can glide as far as 200 feet (about 60 meters) and reach speeds of 20 miles (about 32 kilometers) an hour when moving from tree to tree in its forest home. All of its gliding is done at night, for the flying squirrel is a nocturnal creature. It spends the day sleeping in a leaf-lined nest within a hollow tree. When it ventures out at night, it goes in search of food—berries, tree buds, seeds, nuts—and water. Once a year, a female flying squirrel produces from three to six babies—tiny, hairless creatures with transparent flying membranes. By the time a young flying squirrel is 12 weeks old, it is gliding as expertly as its parents. It seems to be born with an instinctive knowledge of this complex skill.

Red Fox

"As cunning as a fox"—people sometimes use this phrase to describe a person who is especially crafty or clever, someone very good at outwitting others. The comparison is an appropriate one, for the fox *is* an unusually sharp-witted animal. The red fox (*Vulpes fulva*), which is found throughout much of North America, exhibits all the cleverness that is typical of the whole

fox family. When chased by an enemy— whether it is a bobcat, a wolf, or a hunting dog—the red fox is skilled at disguising its own trail. It uses such methods as running in circles, cutting back and forth across a stream, and even walking along the top of a fence or a wall to confuse its pursuers. When playing the part of the hunter rather than the hunted, the red fox also displays intelligence and cunning. Silently approaching an unsuspecting mouse or rabbit, the fox pounces on its victim before it has a chance to escape. The red fox also uses its hunting skills to catch birds, snakes, and insects, as well as an occasional porcupine. Young foxes, called *kits*, learn how to hunt by following the example of their parents; they begin their lessons when they are about 12 weeks old. The fox family—mother, father, and four to ten kits—stays together until the youngsters are able to take care of themselves. Then each animal sets out on its own to face the dangers and the opportunities of its environment.

Koala

Of all the animals of the woodland, the koala (*Phascolarctos cinereus*) is the one whose way of life is most dependent on the trees of the woodland environment. This unique animal makes its home in the eucalyptus forests of eastern Australia, and it spends almost its entire lifetime amid the leaves and branches of the tall eucalyptus trees. The silvery-gray eucalyptus leaves are the koala's only food; the juice in the leaves and the dew that covers them are its only sources of moisture. Koalas do most of their eating and drinking during the hours of darkness. They spend the night feeding on the juicy eucalyptus leaves, climbing from branch to branch with the aid of their strong, flexible fingers and toes. During the day, koalas usually sleep curled up in the fork of a tree branch.

The branches of the eucalyptus tree serve not only as the koala's bedroom and kitchen but also as its nursery, for the female koala gives birth to her babies within their leafy shelter. Like the kangaroo and the opossum, the koala is a *marsupial*—a mammal that carries its young in a pouch after they are born. The young koala, like other marsupial babies, is only partially developed at birth. It is very small—only three-quarters of an inch (about two centimeters) long—and it cannot see or hear. Immediately after birth, the tiny creature crawls into its mother's pouch, which is located low on the front of her body. There it spends the first five or six months of its life, drinking its mother's milk and continuing its development. Even after the young koala finally ventures out of the pouch, it stays with its mother for almost a year, clinging to her back as she climbs in the trees or nestling against her as she sleeps. After this period of slow development, the youngster is ready to join the other koalas in their endless search for the eucalyptus leaves on which their lives depend.

Beaver

Beavers are builders. Out of the trees of the woodlands they make remarkably sturdy dams and cozy, well-protected houses. A beaver's mud-plastered house, called a *lodge*, is usually located in the midst of a pond or a stream or along its shore. The lodge's dome-shaped roof rises high above the surrounding water, which is kept at a constant level by the dam that beavers build out of branches and mud. The clever beaver, largest of North American rodents, is well equipped for its work as a tree cutter, carpenter, and underwater engineer. Its four large front teeth have chisel-like edges that can quickly cut through the trunks of small trees. When a beaver cuts down a tree, it stands on its hind legs and uses its paddle-shaped tail as a prop. Other parts of the beaver's body serve equally useful purposes. Its hind feet are webbed for efficient swimming, while its clawed front feet are good for grasping and arranging building materials. A beaver's coat is made up of an outer layer of long, coarse hair and an inner layer of short, soft hair, both of which serve to keep the animal warm in the coldest water. During a good part of the year, beavers spend many hours in the water, building and repairing their dams and lodges or storing their winter food supply of bark and twigs. In preparation for winter, beavers drag branches of their favorite trees—aspens, cottonwoods, willows—to the bottom of the pond. They anchor the branches near the underwater entrances of their lodges so that when the pond freezes over, they will be able to swim out of their warm, dry homes and enjoy a winter meal under the ice. When the ice on the pond melts in the spring, the female beaver brings forth her new offspring—two to four baby beavers, known as *kits*. The kits will live with their parents until they are two years old. Then the adult beavers will drive the youngsters away to make room for that year's new additions to the family.

White-tailed Deer

Of the three species of deer found in the United States, the white-tailed deer (*Odocoileus virginianus*) is probably the most numerous and the most familiar. The distinctive white tail markings that give this deer its name can be seen only when the animal is in flight, bounding through the underbrush of the woodland. When the white-tailed deer flees from danger, it flips its tail up, revealing the white underside that serves as a warning signal

to other deer. When the animal stands quietly, its tail is lowered, and only the reddish-brown upper surface can be seen. At rest or in flight, the white-tailed deer is a graceful creature very much at home among the trees of the woodland environment. The bark, twigs, and leaves of trees such as the cedar and the spruce make up a large part of the deer's food supply. The woodland trees also provide the white-tailed deer with shelter from summer sun and winter wind. And the dried leaves and grasses of the forest floor serve as a bed for the young deer, or fawns, who are born each spring. For the first month of its life, a fawn lies almost motionless in its grassy bed, its white-spotted coat blending with the forest pattern of sun and shadow. During this time, the mother deer comes frequently to feed her helpless baby and to check on its safety. Soon the young deer is strong enough to leave its hiding place and to follow its mother as she wanders through the forest, searching for food.

Moose

The moose (*Alces alces*), largest member of the deer family, is an animal with a very distinctive appearance. Both male and female moose have long, bulb-shaped muzzles, humped shoulders, and dangling flaps of skin, called *bells*, hanging from their throats. The males, or bulls, boast an additional outstanding feature—a set of heavy, branching antlers, nearly four feet (about 1.2 meters) in width. The antlers are used as weapons once a year during the fall mating season, when the bull moose battle with each other for the privilege of mating with the females, or cows. After mating season is over, the antlers are shed, to be replaced by a new set that begins to develop in the spring. It is also in the spring that the moose calves are born— wooly-coated little creatures, often twins,

each weighing about 25 pounds (about 11.3 kilograms). As soon as the calves are strong enough, they follow their mothers to forest lakes and streams in search of food. Moose, who are excellent swimmers, eat many kinds of plants that grow in or near bodies of water. They are particularly fond of water lilies, which make up a good part of their summer diet. In order to obtain this favorite food, a moose will wade into a forest lake and dive to the bottom, coming up with a mouthful of water-lily stems and roots. The animal also feeds on the leaves and twigs of trees such as willows, aspens, pines, and birches. In fact, the moose's common English name comes from the Algonquin Indian word *musee*, which means "wood-eater." This name, however, is common only in North America; in Europe, members of the genus *Alces* are called "elk." To make things even more confusing, Americans have borrowed the name *elk* and use it to refer to the wapiti (*Cervus canadensis*), a native American animal related to the moose.

Otter

Most wild animals are playful when they are young, but otters play all of their lives. The North American otter (genus *Lutra*), a member of the weasel family, spends many hours of its adult life frolicking in the waters of woodland lakes and streams. Otters indulge in a wide range of water games: shooting rapids, diving for clam shells, playing tag, sliding down snow-covered banks into icy-cold streams. These sleek brown mammals are as much at home in water as on land. Their streamlined bodies, tapered tails, and webbed feet enable them to move swiftly in the water, not only when playing but also when pursuing food. An otter's diet consists largely of creatures that make their homes in streams and lakes—crayfish, mussels, and fish, as well as frogs and other amphibians. The otter lives close to its source of food and entertainment, usually in a den dug into a streambank. The den, lined with dried grass and twigs, is the birthplace of the two to four babies that a female otter bears each year. Baby otters are born blind, and they remain blind until they are about two months old. When the young otters are ready to face the world outside their den, the mother otter teaches them the essential art of swimming.

Scale of Animal Sizes

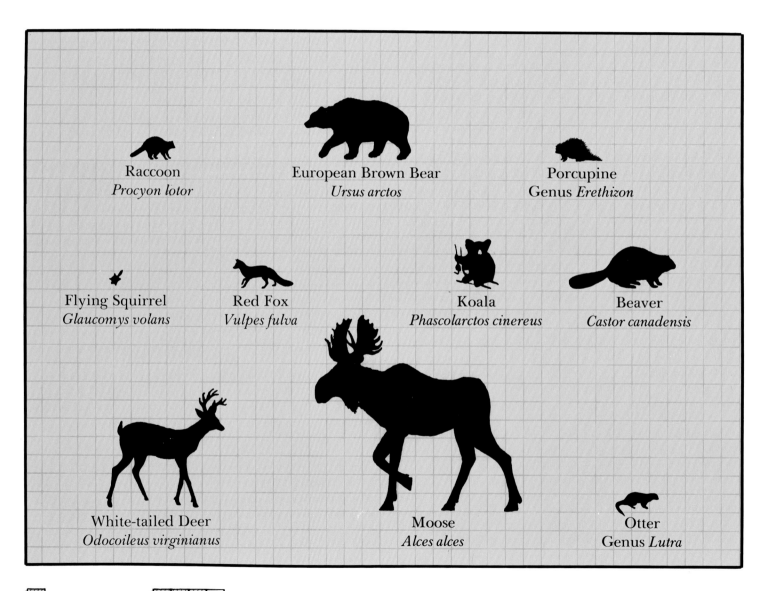

Raccoon
Procyon lotor

European Brown Bear
Ursus arctos

Porcupine
Genus *Erethizon*

Flying Squirrel
Glaucomys volans

Red Fox
Vulpes fulva

Koala
Phascolarctos cinereus

Beaver
Castor canadensis

White-tailed Deer
Odocoileus virginianus

Moose
Alces alces

Otter
Genus *Lutra*

 = *1 Foot*    = *1 Meter*

Animals of the Temperate Forests